THE JEWISH CHILDREN'S BIBLE
LEVITICUS

Adapted by Sheryl Prenzlau

PITSPOPANY

NEW YORK ◆ JERUSALEM

Aaron blessing the people.

Also available in **THE JEWISH CHILDREN'S BIBLE** series:
GENESIS
EXODUS with *The Children's Haggadah*
NUMBERS with *The Book of Ruth*
DEUTERONOMY with *The Book of Jonah*

Published by Pitspopany Press
Text copyright © 1999 by Sheryl Prenzlau
Illustrations copyright © 1999 by Zely Smekhov

Design: Benjie Herskowitz

PITSPOPANY PRESS books may be purchased for educational or special sales by contacting:
Marketing Director, Pitspopany Press, 40 East 78th Street, Suite 16D, New York, New York 10021. Fax: 212 472-6253.

ISBN: 0-943706-33-5

Printed in Hong Kong

Contents

Continued on next page

Contents

Continued from previous page

God Calls Moses ויקרא

The *mishkan,* the House of God, was now standing. It was built exactly as God had required, and it was perfect in every way. It was an awesome place, filled with the Presence of God. In fact, it was so awesome, that Moses was afraid to enter it. But God wanted Moses to know that this place was built for the people, too. So God called to Moses from the mishkan and began to tell him what the mishkan would be used for.

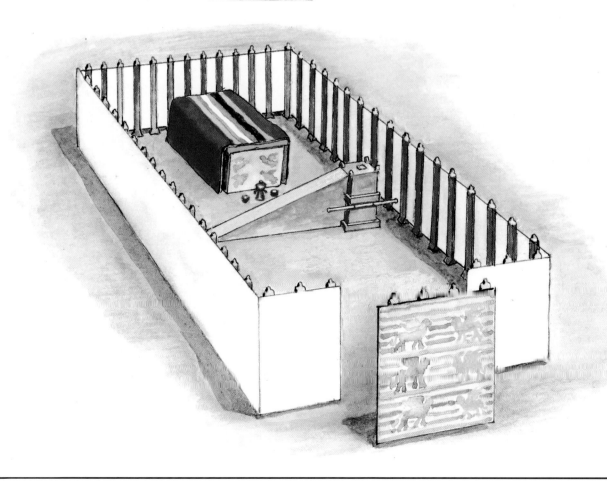

The Animal Sacrifices

"Moses," God said, "speak to the Children of Israel and tell them that when a person offers a sacrifice in the mishkan it should be an animal sacrifice."

Then God described to Moses how to bring the different kinds of sacrifices. Sometimes people would have to bring cattle, goats,

sheep, or birds for the sacrifice. The Kohanim were to perform the sacrifices. They were told how to sacrifice each offering to God, and what part they would receive from each offering. An important ingredient in all sacrifices was salt.

The Rising Offering

If someone had bad thoughts, or if he didn't do a commandment he was supposed to do, then he could bring a Rising Offering. This offering was completely burnt on the altar to show that it was all for God.

The Peace Offering

If a person wanted to express his love for God, he would bring a Peace Offering. This was the way to show how happy you were for what God had done for you.

The best parts of the animal would be burnt on the altar. The rest of the animal was eaten by the Kohanim and any pure person, in Jerusalem.

The Sin Offering

If a person carelessly did something that he shouldn't have done, he would bring a Sin Offering. Being careless about the commandments in the Torah meant you were being lazy or not paying attention. The Sin Offering would show that you were asking forgiveness from God.

In certain cases a person would bring his Sin Offering according to what he could afford. If he couldn't afford a large animal, he would bring a small animal. If he couldn't afford a small animal, he would bring birds, which were less expensive to buy. If he couldn't afford birds, he would bring flour.

This Sin Offering was brought when:
A person swore to tell the truth and then lied unintentionally.
A person forgot he touched a dead body and then ate from holy food in the mishkan.
A person swore he would do something but then forgot to do it. Or if he swore something happened, but it didn't.

Three Special Sins

There were three special Sin Offerings that were brought, when:
The Kohen Gadol, called the High Priest in English, committed a careless sin.
The Sanhedrin HaGadol, called the Great Court in English, told the people to do something they shouldn't, and the people did what the court said.
The Ruler carelessly committed a sin.

The Guilt Offering

A person had to bring a Guilt Offering when:
He was not sure if he committed certain sins.
For instance, if there were two pieces of matzah on Passover, and a person ate one of the pieces. Later, he learned that one of them was not kosher for Passover.
He stole property from another person.

The Meal Offering

Sometimes a person wanted to bring a sacrifice just to get close to God. This was called a Meal Offering. The ingredients for a Meal Offering were flour, oil, and a spice called frankincense.

The Kohen's Job   צו

God told Moses exactly what the Kohanim should do with all of the different sacrifices. Some sacrifices were to be offered on the altar and then parts of the animal were to be given to the Kohanim to eat. Some sacrifices had to be burnt completely on the altar. Some sacrifices could only be eaten by the Kohen who helped bring the sacrifice. Other sacrifices could be eaten by any Kohen.

Some sacrifices could be eaten by the person who brought it, as well as by his family and friends.

Some sacrifices could be eaten for two days. And some had to be finished that very same day.

The Thanksgiving Offering

When someone wanted to thank God for saving his life, or for keeping him out of danger, he would bring a Thanksgiving Offering. This offering consisted of a Peace Offering plus 40 loaves of bread.

Kosher Pots

God told Moses to tell Aaron and his sons that if something non-kosher is cooked in a kosher clay pot, then the pot has to be broken. It can't be used again. But if something non-kosher is cooked in a metal pot, then the pot can be cleaned and used again.

Fat And Blood

God told Moses that when an animal is sacrificed, the people have to be careful not to eat the special fat that is brought on the altar.

All blood from animals is forbidden. This includes the blood of birds, but not of fish.

God explained why it is forbidden to drink blood. "For the soul of the flesh is in the blood." The blood is what keeps the animal living. The blood represents the life of the animal.

If a person eats the fat or the blood that is forbidden, he will be cut off from the people, by God.

Aaron And His Sons Become Kohanim – Officially

Moses was told to gather all the people in front of the mishkan. There, he took Aaron and his sons and immersed them in a special body of water called a *mikvah*. Then Moses dressed Aaron and his sons with the special Priestly clothing. He took oil and anointed Aaron. Finally, Moses sacrificed a Sin Offering, a Rising Offering, and a special Peace Offering to God.

Aaron and his sons ate from the Peace Offering. For seven days they stayed at the mishkan. They were given the job of protecting the mishkan by doing all the work that had to be done there for God.

Aaron And His Sons   שמיני
Begin Their Jobs – Officially

For seven days, Aaron and his sons worked in the mishkan. On the eighth day the mishkan was officially opened.

All the people gathered. God commanded Aaron and his sons to bring special sacrifices to celebrate this wonderful day. After the sacrifices were completed, Aaron blessed the people. Then both Moses and Aaron blessed the people.

The spirit of God came down onto the mishkan. A fire came out of the Holy of Holies in the mishkan and burned up the Rising Offering and the fats that Aaron had brought to be sacrificed.

Nadav And Avihu Sin

Two of Aaron's sons, Nadav and Avihu, brought incense into the mishkan when they weren't supposed to. This was a great sin. God sent a bolt of fire to kill them.

Aaron was very sad. Moses told Aaron that even though Nadav and Avihu had sinned, they were great people and God loved them. This comforted Aaron and he was able to continue his work.

Moses called to two of Aaron's cousins to bring out the bodies of Nadav and Avihu from the mishkan.

Because of the importance of this day, Aaron and his two remaining sons were not allowed to show any signs of mourning.

A Special Law For Aaron And His Sons

God told Aaron that a Kohen is forbidden to drink wine or other alcoholic drinks while he is in the mishkan. A Kohen always has to be able to tell between what is holy and what is not holy. If he drinks wine or liquor he could make a mistake.

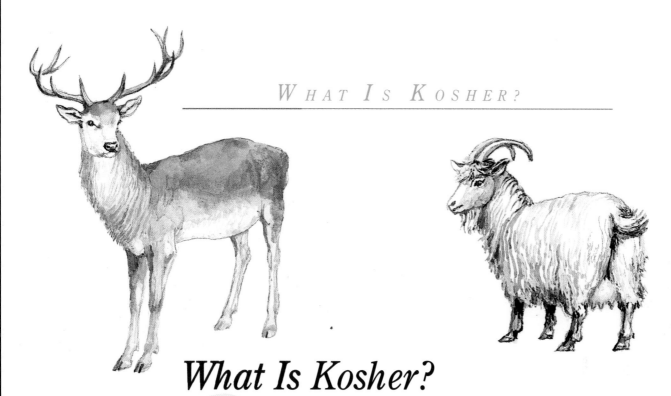

What Is Kosher?

God told Moses and Aaron. "Tell the Children of Israel that these are the living things that you are allowed to eat."

Animals: You can eat animals that have completely split hooves and that chew their cud. *Chewing cud is when the animal brings up chewed food from its stomach in order to chew it into finer pieces.* But if the animal only has one of these signs, like the pig, which has split hooves but does not chew its cud, then you cannot eat that animal.

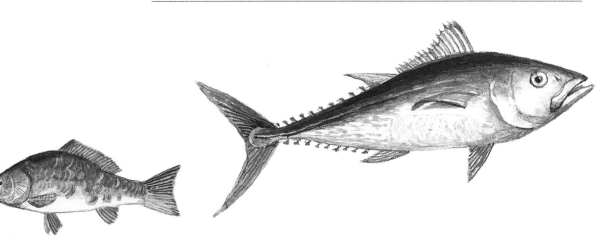

Fish: You can eat fish that have fins and scales in the water.

Birds: You cannot eat certain birds, like the eagle or the bat. But the Torah does not list the birds that you can eat. A person can eat the birds which are known in his community to be kosher.

Insects: You cannot eat insects such as flies, bees, beetles, centipedes, and mosquitos.

Why Kosher?

God said that the reason for eating kosher is so "you will make yourselves holy, as I am holy." God did not want the people to eat things that would prevent them from reaching a high level of holiness.

God reminded the people that "I am the One who took you out of Egypt to be your God, and I want you to be holy, for I am holy."

The Disease Of Tzaraat תזריע

One of the jobs of the Kohen was to check if someone had tzaraat. This was a disease that infected people who spoke evil of others. It infected a person's skin, but it could also infect a person's clothing and even the walls of his house.

If a person found a spot on his skin, he would go to the Kohen. The Kohen would look to see if the person's skin and hair had changed color and become very white. If the Kohen wasn't sure whether the spot was tzaraat, he would tell the person to come back in seven days.

If, after seven days, the Kohen found that the person had tzaraat, then the person had to:

Tear his clothing like a mourner.

Let his hair grow like a mourner.

Put a scarf over his mouth.

Tell everyone to stay away from him.

When the tzaraat went away, the person had to go through a special ceremony to make him pure. Then he could enter the camp again.

Tzaraat Of Clothing

If any part of a person's clothing began to change color, he had to bring it to the Kohen. The Kohen would see whether the color was green or red. If it was, then the Kohen would put the clothing aside for seven days.

If, after seven days, the color had spread, it was tzaraat. The clothing had to be burned. If the color stayed the same, the clothing had to be washed and then put aside for another week.

At the end of the second week, if the color still looked the same, the clothing had to be burned. If the color became lighter, the person could cut the spot out and then use the garment.

Tzaraat מצורע Of A House

If a person thought his house had tzaraat, he would have to tell the Kohen that something strange was happening to his house. Then he had to take everything out of his house and call the Kohen to have a look. If the Kohen found red or green colors on the walls, which were not there before, the Kohen would close up the house for seven days.

If, after seven days, the colors were still on the stones, those stones would be removed and new stones put in their place. But if the red or green color spread to other stones, then the house had to be torn down. It was a house of tzaraat.

When The Tzaraat Disappeared

When the tzaraat on a person disappeared, he had to bring a Bird Offering. A second bird was set free in a field by the Kohen. The person who was now free of tzaraat had to wash his clothing and himself in a mikvah, and shave. Seven days later the Kohen had to shave off all the person's hair on his head and face. Then the person had to wash his clothing and himself in a mikvah again. On the eighth day, he had to bring animal sacrifices.

The Yom Kippur Service אחרי מות

After the sons of Aaron died, God explained exactly when and how Aaron could come into the Holy of Holies in the mishkan.

Aaron, as the Kohen Gadol, could go into the Holy of Holies only on Yom Kippur. He had special white clothing that was worn only on Yom Kippur. He had to bring a Sin Offering for himself and his family. He also had to bring two male goats as part of the Yom Kippur service.

God declared Yom Kippur to be a day of atonement forever. It was called the "Sabbath of Sabbaths," a day of complete rest.

The Two Goats

Aaron took the two goats in front of the Tent of Meeting. He put two lots in a box. One said "For God" and the other said "For Azazel." Without looking into the box, Aaron took out one lot and put it on the head of one goat. Then he took out the other lot and put it on the head of the second goat.

The goat that had the "For God" lot on his head was sacrificed to God. Aaron put his hands on the "Azazel" goat and confessed all the sins of the people. Then this goat was led out into the desert and killed.

Whom You Can't Marry

God told Moses that the Children of Israel should not do the disgusting things they saw in Egypt or will see in Canaan. God said, "Observe My decrees and My laws to carry them out so that you will live by them – I am God."

Then God listed the relatives a person can't marry, including a mother, father, sister, and brother. God also listed the other types of marriages that are forbidden, including marrying someone who is already married.

What Happens If You Disobey

God warned the people that if they do the terrible things that other nations do, the Land of Israel will become diseased. It will have no choice but to throw the Children of Israel out.

"Therefore," God told the people, "keep My decrees and laws, and don't do the terrible things that those who came onto the Land before you did. So that the Land will not throw you out. I am God."

How To Become Holy קדושים

God told Moses, "Tell the Children of Israel to be holy because I, your God, am Holy." Then God gave the people a number of rules that would help them to become holy.

ༀ Have awe (fear) of your parents.

ༀ Keep the Sabbath.
ༀ Do not worship idols.
ༀ Give part of your harvest to the poor.
ༀ Do not steal or lie.
ༀ Do not swear falsely using God's Name.
ༀ Do not hold back the money you owe someone who works for you.
ༀ Do not curse a deaf person or place an obstacle in front of a blind person.
ༀ If you're a judge, do not favor one person more than another.
ༀ Do not gossip.
ༀ Do not keep a grudge. Tell the person what he can do to set things right.

  ℝ Do not take revenge.
  ℝ Love your fellow man as you love yourself.

  ℝ Do not wear linen and wool together in a garment.
  ℝ When you plant a fruit tree in the Land of Israel, do not eat the tree's fruit for three years. On the fourth year you are to eat the fruits in Jerusalem. On the fifth year you can eat the fruits wherever you want to.
  ℝ Do not perform witchcraft.
  ℝ Stand up when an old person enters the room and honor a wise man.
  ℝ Do not make fun of a person who converts to Judaism. Love him like yourself.
  ℝ Do not cheat in your business.

If the people do these commandments, then the Land of Israel will be flowing with milk and honey.

Rules For A Kohen אמור

A Kohen has to be holy. He cannot go near a dead body except if the dead person is his mother, father, son, daughter, brother, unmarried sister, or wife. He can only attend the funeral of these seven members of his family. A Kohen Gadol can't attend the funeral of anyone. After all, he goes into the mishkan all the time and must remain holy.

A Kohen can't marry a divorced woman. A Kohen Gadol can't marry a widow or a divorced woman.

Who Can Eat Terumah

A Kohen and his family ate *terumah*. This was the food given to them from the Children of Israel. It was considered holy food. Someone visiting the Kohen was not allowed to eat terumah. But the Kohen's servant was permitted to eat terumah.

If a non-Kohen ate terumah by accident, he had to give back the worth of what he ate and add one-fifth of the value of what he had eaten.

Animals For Sacrifices

God said, "When an ox or a sheep or a goat is born, it must remain with its mother for seven days. From the eighth day, it can be used as a sacrifice. But you cannot slaughter the mother and child on the same day."

An animal that had something wrong with it could not be used for a sacrifice. For instance, if the animal was blind, or had a skin disease, or one limb longer than the other, it could not be used for a sacrifice.

The Jewish Holidays

God told Moses to tell the people about the Jewish holidays. With each holiday, certain sacrifices had to be brought.

The Sabbath: "For six days work may be done, and on the seventh day there should be rest. You should not do any work."

Pesach: "On the 15th day of this month (Nissan) is the Festival of Matzah to God. You should eat matzah for seven days. You should not work on the first and last day of the holiday."

Shavuot: "When you enter the Land of Israel and you reap the harvest, bring an omer (a certain amount of barley) from your first harvest to the Kohen." Until a person brought his omer, which was on the second day of Pesach, he could not eat of his harvest. From that day he began counting toward the holiday of Shavuot. The counting took seven weeks. Shavuot was on the 50th day. No work was to be done.

Rosh Hashanah: "On the first day of the seventh month (Tishray) you should rest. It is a remembrance day, with shofar blasts. You should not do any work."

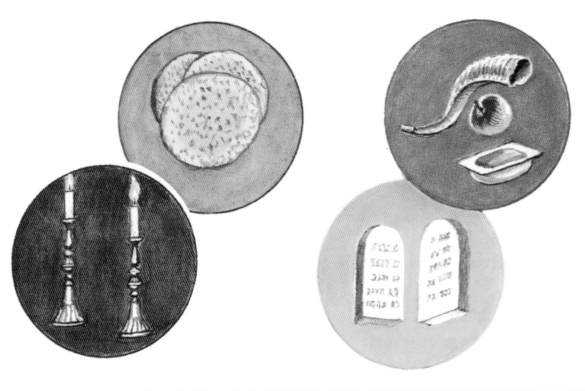

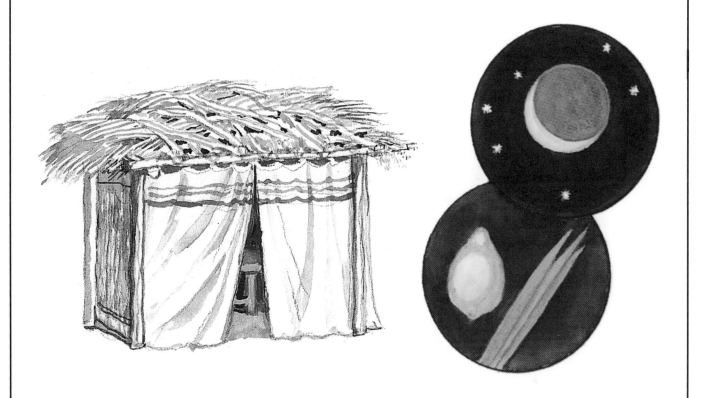

Yom Kippur, called The Day of Atonement, is observed ten days after Rosh Hashanah. The people have to fast and should not work. "For any person who will not fast on this day will be cut off from the people."

Sukkot: "On the 15th of the seventh month is the Festival of Sukkot. It is a seven-day holiday. On the first day you should not do any work." The people were told to take a lulav, etrog, hadasim (myrtle branches), and aravot (willow branches) in order to "rejoice before God."

"You should live in booths," God said, "so that your children will know that I had the Children of Israel live in booths when I took them out of Egypt."

The day after Sukkot is called **Shemini Atzeret.** No work is to be done on this day.

Two Special Jobs For The Kohanim

A Kohen had to light the gold menorah in the mishkan every evening. Clear olive oil had to be used to light the menorah.

Every Friday, 12 large loaves of bread were baked by the Kohanim. Two stacks of six loaves each were placed on the table in the mishkan on the Sabbath. The Kohanim ate the bread on the following Sabbath.

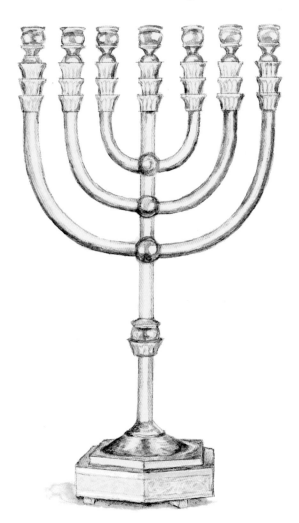

The Man Who Cursed God

When the Children of Israel were in Egypt, Shlomit the daughter of Divri, had a son from an Egyptian man. In the desert, her son had a fight with one of the men in the camp. During the fight Shlomit's son said the special Name of God and then cursed God.

This is called blaspheming God. The people who heard him brought him to Moses.

Moses placed the blasphemer in jail. He wanted to know what to do with him.

God spoke to Moses, saying, "Take the blasphemer outside the camp. All those who heard him should put their hands on his head. Then they should stone him."

God explained that anyone who blasphemes God must be put to death. And not only that, but if someone kills another person he must be put to death.

But if someone kills another person's animal, he only has to pay money to the owner of the animal. This is also true if a person wounds someone, or takes out an eye or a tooth of someone. He must pay the person he injured.

Shemittah

בהר

God told Moses that when the people entered the Land they would be able to work the Land for six years. But the seventh year was a Sabbath for the Land. It was called *shemittah*. A person could not plant or harvest his field during the seventh year. Also during the seventh year, anyone could eat from anyone else's land.

"If you ask," God says, "what will we eat on the seventh year if we can't plant and harvest? I, God, will give your land a blessing on the sixth year so that it will grow all that you need for the seventh, eighth, and ninth year."

Yovel

After seven shemittah years, 49 years in total, the 50th year was to be a Jubilee Year. It was called *yovel*. On Yom Kippur of the Jubilee Year the shofar would be blown throughout the Land of Israel. In this year it would also be forbidden to plant or harvest, and everyone could eat from the fields.

But in the Jubilee Year not only would the Land rest, but everyone would get back the land of his inheritance. That meant that a person who sold his land right after yovel would automatically get it back 50 years later.

All Jews who became slaves of others Jews because they could not pay their debts, had to be freed on the Jubilee Year. Then these poor Jews could go home to the land of their inheritance as free men.

God also warned the people that they must never treat Jews as slaves. Even if they are sold into slavery, they must be treated as workers. "For the Children of Israel are servants to Me," God says. "They are My servants whom I have taken out of the land of Egypt."

The Blessings בחוקותי

God told the people their reward for doing the commandments.

"I will give you rain at the right time and the Land will bear fruit. Everyone will eat their full and live in safety. When the enemies come, 5 Jewish soldiers will chase 100 of the enemy, and 100 Jewish soldiers will chase 10,000 of the enemy."

Not only that, but God would also make the Jewish people numerous. "I will walk among you," God adds, "I will be your God and you will be My people."

The Curses

"But if you will not listen to Me," God warned, "and don't do my commandments. And if you treat my laws with disgust, I will treat you the same way."

There will be disease, and the enemy will overrun the Land of Israel. And if the people still won't listen to God, even worse punishments will happen. The clouds won't let the rain fall and the people, starving and thirsty, will be forced to live among the other nations.

"But despite all this," God said, "when the people are in the land of their enemies, I won't reject them or destroy them. I won't cancel my agreement with them."

Gifts To The Temple

If a man swore to give the worth of himself or another person to the Temple, he had to give a set amount according to the age and sex of that person. For example, if someone swore to give the worth of a 20-year-old male to the Temple, he had to give 50 silver shekels.

If a man swore to give a specific kosher animal to the Temple, he was not allowed to change his mind and give a different animal. If a man wanted to give the worth of a non-kosher animal to the Temple, he had to give the worth of the animal plus an additional one-fifth.

A man could also give the worth of his house or his field to the mishkan. The amount he had to pay was based on the yovel. The Kohen would figure out how many years were left until the yovel and how much the field or house was worth during that period of time.

Different Tithes

A person had to eat one-tenth of his crop in Jerusalem. If he wanted to, he could sell his crop and then take the money and buy food in Jerusalem. The food had to be eaten in Jerusalem.

A person had to bring every tenth newborn kosher animal to the Temple. There, it was sacrificed and the meat eaten by the owner.

Fulfillment Of A Promise

God reminded the Children of Israel that if they obey the commandments, then the promises that God made to Jacob, Isaac, and Abraham would be fulfilled.

MIDRASHIM
TALES OF OUR SAGES

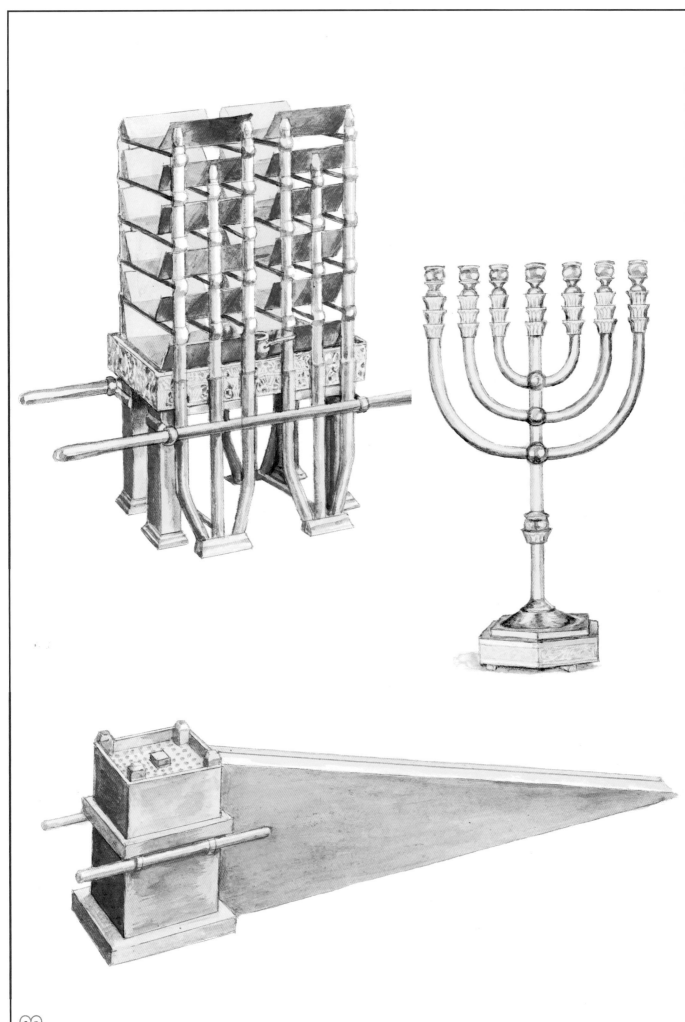

ויקרא

The Book of Leviticus is also called Torat Kohanim, "the Laws of the Priests," since most of the laws in it pertain directly to the Priests. But all of the Children of Israel are required to learn it, even those who are not Kohanim. Why? Because learning about the sacrifices is a substitute for not being able to bring sacrifices anymore. When we learn the Torah, God counts it as if we had actually brought the sacrifices to the Temple.

Salt is added to every sacrifice that is burnt on the altar. Why is this? The midrash tells us that during Creation, God separated the waters of heaven from the waters of earth. The earthly waters complained, saying, "But we also want to be close to you, God." God compensated the earthly waters by giving them a part in the Temple Service. Salt, which comes from the sea, would be added to each sacrifice that is burnt on the altar.

If someone wants to express his love for God, he can bring a Peace Offering. Why does this particular offering symbolize peace?

This is the only offering that is enjoyed by everyone. The inner organs of the animal are placed on the altar for God, the breast and thigh of the animal go to the Kohen, and the one who brings the sacrifice gets the skin and the rest of the meat. We find that God, the Kohen, and the one bringing the sacrifice all receive a portion of the animal. When everything is in harmony, and everyone is content, then it is possible to have true peace.

צו

The Thanksgiving Offering was only brought when a person felt extreme gratitude to God for saving him from a specific tragedy. There were four situations when this offering was brought:

- Upon surviving a dangerous journey through the desert.

 ☙ Upon release from prison.
 ☙ After having recovered from a serious illness.
 ☙ After crossing the sea.

Today, instead of bringing a Thanksgiving Offering in these instances, we thank God in a different manner. On the first Monday, Thursday, or Sabbath that a person comes to synagogue after one of these situations, he says the special "Hagomel" blessing, thanking God for helping him.

The Torah tells us that anyone who eats the fat or blood of the sacrificed animal will be "cut off" from the people. In Hebrew, the word which represents this is *karet*.

What does it mean to be cut off? There are some commentaries who say that someone who receives karet will live to see his children die. Others believe that God will shorten the sinner's life and that he will die by the age of 50.

The Ramban believes that just as there are different levels of sinning, there are also different levels of karet. For him, the worst level of karet is the loss of a person's share in the Next World.

שמיני

When he began his work in the mishkan, Aaron was commanded to bring different sacrifices. He had to bring two Sin Offerings – a calf and a goat.

Why were two different animals used for this?

The midrash notes that each of these Sin Offerings was symbolic, and came to atone for two earlier sins.

Aaron sacrificed a calf in order to atone for making the Golden Calf for the nation.

The goat was sacrificed to atone for what Joseph's brothers had done to their father, Jacob. After selling Joseph, his brothers slaughtered a goat and dipped Joseph's coat in the blood. When they showed the coat to Jacob, he thought that his son had been killed by a wild animal.

The sages have different explanations about what sin Nadav and Avihu committed, that resulted in God killing them.

One explanation is that they drank too much wine at the celebration, and entered the mishkan drunk.

Another explanation is that they decided to light the fire on their own, and didn't ask permission from Moses or Aaron.

Yet others say that they entered the Holy of Holies, where only the High Priest may enter (and only once a year on Yom Kippur).

But most of the authorities agree that the brothers' sin was that they brought a fire with them into the mishkan, instead of waiting for God to send a fire that would consume the incense. By doing so, they showed their lack of faith in God.

Some of the laws of what is and what is not kosher are written specifically in the Torah, while others are extrapolated.

For example: Kosher fish must have fins and scales "in the water." From this verse we learn that if a fish has fins and scales in the water, but sheds its scales when it leaves the water (as some fish do), it is still a kosher fish.

The Rabbis give various reasons for these laws.

One reason is that God knows which animals prevent us from reaching a higher spiritual level. God is telling us to eat only those animals which will bring us closer to our own Godly nature.

Another reason is that while most kosher animals are domestic, most non-kosher animals are predators. God does not want us to be like predators.

תזריע

Why does a person with tzaraat have to live away from everyone else? After all, tzaraat is not contagious.

Rashi tells us that tzaraat comes from speaking evil about others. When someone speaks evil about someone, he often causes others to shun the person he is talking about. So now, when he gets tzaraat, the evil speaker is separated from everyone.

Hopefully, when he experiences how it feels to be shunned, he will think twice before putting others in this position.

ﬁ

Someone with tzaraat on his body has to be sent out of the camp. But, someone whose entire body is covered by tzaraat can remain in the camp. Why is that?

Rabbi S. R. Hirsch points out that tzaraat should not be confused with leprosy. It is a disease given by God for a specific sin that is committed. The clearest difference between the two diseases is the fact that a person with head-to-toe tzaraat can come into the camp, whereas a person whose body was covered with leprosy would be considered too contagious to go into the camp.

ﬁ

מצורע

The people were told to empty their houses of all their belongings before calling the Kohen to check if their house had tzaraat. Why is this?

The midrash says that if a person was stingy, his house would get tzaraat. For instance, if his neighbor asked to borrow a hammer, the owner of the house would say, "Sorry, I don't have a hammer." But when his house contracted tzaraat, he would be forced to remove his belongings from his house. Then, everyone would clearly see that he had a hammer, and was just being stingy.

ﬁ

In case of tzaraat, there are three places on the body where the hair is completely shaven off: head, beard and eyebrows. This is in order to atone, in part, for three of the reasons that a person receives tzaraat.

The first reason is arrogance. An arrogant person feels that he is the best, head and shoulders above the rest. That's why his

head is shaven.

The second reason is speaking evil about others. Since his mouth was used to speak evil, the hair surrounding the mouth is shaven.

The third reason is the person's inability to see any good in other people. That is why the hair surrounding his eyes is shaven.

אחרי מות

"Observe my decrees and my laws so that you will live by them."

From the words "and live by them," we learn that – with the exception of murder, adultery, and idolatry – a person can transgress all the commandments in the Bible in order to save his life. God would rather that we live to fulfill the commandments than die because of them.

God tells the Jewish nation that if they don't follow God's path, the Land will throw them out.

The Land of Israel is more than just an inanimate object. It lives and breathes the Jewish people. It can be compared to a human body. As long as you eat good, healthy food, you will be able to function normally, but once you eat something spoiled you will get sick and throw it up.

The Land of Israel is much the same. As long as the Jewish people behave properly on the Land, they can live in harmony. But when they begin to act improperly, the Land becomes sick and throws them out!

קדושים

Why does the Torah place the mother ahead of the father in the commandment to have awe (fear) of parents? And why,

when the Torah talks about honoring parents, is the father placed before the mother?

Rashi tells us that the natural tendency of a person is to fear his father more than his mother. That's why, when it comes to awe/fear, the Torah emphasizes the mother first. However, when it comes to honor, a person tends to honor his mother more than his father. So, when the Torah speaks of honor, it mentions the father ahead of the mother.

We are told "Love your fellow man as you love yourself."

The corollary to this rule was voiced by the great sage, Hillel.

A man once approached Hillel, and asked to be taught the entire Torah while standing on one foot!

Hillel replied, "What you would hate done to you, don't do unto others. That is the basis of the entire Torah."

אמור

What caused the son of Shlomit to blaspheme God?

One explanation is based on the fact that the tribe a man belonged to was determined by his father. Shlomit was from the tribe of Dan, but her husband had been an Egyptian. This meant that her son had no tribe to belong to. Her son wanted the tribe of Dan to provide him with land as an inheritance. But the leaders of the tribe said they didn't have to give him anything since his father was not from their tribe.

The case was brought to Moses, and he ruled that the tribe of Dan wasn't obligated to give him any land. This made the son of Shlomit so angry, that he cursed God.

But while this man did something terrible, the tribe of Dan were not free of guilt. The leaders of the tribe were told to place their hands on the man's head before he was killed. This was to show that his death was their fault as well. Had

they been more sympathetic, and helped him out, then he wouldn't have been driven to curse God.

בהר

Our Sages tell us that the idea behind the shemittah year is very similar to the concept of the Sabbath.

Just as God created the world in six days and rested on the seventh, so too man must work for six days and rest on the seventh.

During the Sabbath, we have the time we need to fully appreciate the world we live in. We have the perfect opportunity to remember and acknowledge that God created the world, and continues to sustain it.

During the shemittah year, we also have time to acknowledge that the earth belongs to God. We get the opportunity to realize that whether we work the land or let it lie fallow, it is God's Will which determines how much we receive.

בחוקותי

One of the rewards mentioned for obeying God's commandments is our victory in battle. When the enemies come, 5 Jewish soldiers will chase 100 of the enemy, and 100 Jewish soldiers will chase 10,000 of the enemy.

Our Sages point out that the math seems incorrect. If 5 chase 100, then 100 should only be able to chase 2,000, not 10,000!

They explain that this is to show us how people draw strength from one another. If there are 5 people, each one will only be able to chase 20. But if you have 100 working together and giving each other strength and support, then each person will be strong enough to chase 100 people!

God promises "I will remember my agreement with Jacob, Isaac, and Abraham."

Why is the order of the forefathers reversed here? Usually, they are brought down in the chronological order of Abraham, Isaac, and Jacob.

The Midrash says that Jacob is mentioned first because all of his children were *tzadikim* (righteous men). Both Abraham and Isaac had children that didn't follow in God's path.

Each of the Forefathers is nevertheless mentioned, because each one by himself would have been enough to redeem the nation during their times of trouble.

THE BOOK OF
ESTHER

THE BOOK OF ESTHER reveals how the Hand of God guides the destiny of the Jewish people.

THE BOOK OF ESTHER is read on the holiday of Purim. This is a joyous holiday that is celebrated with a great feast, gifts to the poor, and the giving of food to friends. In the synagogue, the Megillah – The Book of Esther– is read. Children and adults dress up in costume as a reminder that things are not always what they seem.

A long time ago, in the land of Persia, there lived a mighty king, Ahashverosh. He ruled over 127 provinces, which was most of the known world.

King Ahashverosh made a party for all the people in his kingdom. The party lasted for 180 days. When the party was over, the king made another party in Shushan, the capital of Persia. He showed off his gold and silver furniture, his fine cotton drapes, and his expensive gold drinking goblets.

He also wanted to show off his beautiful queen, Vashti.

But Vashti was busy at her own party. She was so busy that when the king sent his messengers to fetch her, Vashti refused. This angered the king, and he called his advisors together to help him

decide how to punish Vashti.

"If you let Vashti get away with this," Memuhan, one of the king's advisors, declared, "then before you know it, women everywhere will refuse to listen to their husbands. My king, you should decree that Vashti will no longer be the queen. Make it clear that every man should be the ruler in his house."

The king did as Memuhan advised.

After a while the king missed Vashti, and felt sorry for what he had done. But once the king wrote a decree, even he could not undo it.

The king's servants saw how sad he was. "Why not

have a contest," they suggested. "Let the heads of each province send their most beautiful girls to Shushan. The girl you like the best will be chosen as your new queen."

The king readily agreed and the contest began.

A Jewish man named Mordechai lived in Shushan with his cousin, Hadassah, who was also called Esther. Mordechai had come to Shushan when the King of Babylon forced the Jews to leave Israel.

Esther was very beautiful. She was chosen to enter the contest for the girl most likely to be the next queen. The king's servants took her to the palace, along with many girls from all the provinces. Mordechai told her not to tell anyone she was Jewish.

When the king saw Esther, he fell in love with her, and made her his queen.

About this time, two of the king's trusted servants, Bigtan and Teresh, decided to kill the king. Mordechai, who was waiting in front of the king's palace for news about Esther, overheard their plan to kill King Ahashverosh. He told Esther, who told the king what Mordechai had discovered. Ahashverosh had the two traitors killed. Mordechai's name, along with his deed, was recorded in the king's Book of Deeds.

Soon after this, King Ahashverosh made Haman his chief advisor. When people saw Haman, they would bow down – everyone, that is, except Mordechai. When Haman found out that Mordechai was a Jew, he decided to destroy all the Jews. He held a *pur* – the Persian word for lottery – to decide on which month to kill the Jews.

The month that was picked was Adar, the last month of the year.

Haman went to the king, saying, "There is a certain nation among the peoples of your kingdom who are different from everyone else. Their laws are different, and they don't follow what the king says. Therefore, the king should have them destroyed, and I will pay 10,000 silver coins to make sure they are all killed."

The king took off his official ring and gave it to Haman. "Do with these people as you wish," he said.

Letters were sent to all the provinces telling the people to destroy the Jews on the 13th day of the month of Adar.

When Mordechai realized what was happening, he tore his clothes to show how sad he was. Jews everywhere began mourning and crying.

Mordechai sent a message to Esther, explaining what the king had done and how all the Jews would soon be killed. He begged Esther to go to the king to ask him to save the Jewish people.

Esther sent back a message saying, "No one can approach the king unless he points his golden scepter at them. If I approach the king without his permission, I will be killed!"

Mordechai replied, "If you refuse to help save the Jews, someone else will save us. Who knows? Maybe you were chosen to be queen just so you would be able to save the Jewish people."

Esther realized that Mordechai was right. She sent him a message saying, "Gather all the Jews in Shushan and tell them to fast for three days and nights. I will fast, too. Then I will go to the king. If I die, then I die."

On the third day of her fast, Esther went to the king. When the king saw her, he extended his scepter in her direction.

"What would you like, my queen?" Ahashverosh asked. "I would gladly give you up to half my kingdom."

"If it pleases the king," Esther said, "I would like you and Haman to come to a party that I have prepared."

The king was delighted, and he ordered that Haman join him at the feast prepared by Queen Esther.

Meanwhile, Haman was very happy that everything

was going his way. Things would be perfect if only Mordechai would bow down to him. Zeresh, Haman's wife, knew how to make her husband feel better. "Make a gallows upon which to hang Mordechai," she advised. "Then go speak to the king and convince him to have Mordechai hung."

Haman liked this idea. He called his carpenters to prepare the gallows at once.

That night the king couldn't sleep. So, he had his Book of Deeds read to him. When the story of how Mordechai had saved the king was read to him, Ahashverosh asked, "What great reward was given to

Mordechai for saving my life?"

"Nothing was given to him," the king's servants answered.

Just then, Haman came into the king's waiting room. He wanted to speak to the king about hanging Mordechai. When the king heard that Haman was outside, he asked him to come in.

"Haman," the king asked, "what do you think should be done for the man the king wants to honor?"

Haman, of course, thought the king was talking about him. Who else would the king wish to honor?

"Well," Haman said with a smile, "the man the king wants to honor should wear the royal robe of the king and sit on the king's horse with a royal crown on his head. He should be paraded through the streets of the city. Your most noble officer should announce, 'This

is what is done for the man the king wants to honor!"

Then the king said to Haman, "Hurry, take the clothes and the horse that you spoke about and do everything you suggested for Mordechai the Jew. Don't omit a single honor."

Haman had to lead Mordechai through the streets and declare, "This is what is done for the man the king wants to honor!"

Haman was very upset. He told his wife Zeresh all that had happened.

"If Mordechai is a Jew," Zeresh warned him, realizing her husband was in deep trouble, "then you will certainly fail in anything you want to do to him."

The king's servant arrived and hurried Haman to the party prepared by the queen.

At Queen Esther's feast, Ahashverosh asked again, "What is your wish, Queen Esther? Even if it is up to half my kingdom, I will give it to you."

"If you really want to help me, Your Majesty," Queen Esther began, "please grant me my life, and the life of my people. For we are about to be destroyed."

"Who would do such a thing?" bellowed the king.

"A terrible man," answered the queen. "This wicked Haman!" she cried, pointing.

When Haman heard this, he trembled. The king was so angry, he walked outside for a minute to calm down. Haman tried to beg Esther to save his life. He moved closer and closer to the queen – closer than was permitted by law.

When the king returned, he saw Haman leaning close to the queen and he became doubly angry. "How dare you move so close to my queen!" Ahashverosh shouted.

Just then, the servant Harvona announced that there were gallows which Haman had set up to hang Mordechai.

The king heard this and said, "Hang Haman on it!"

So, Haman was hanged on the gallows he had prepared for Mordechai.

That day, Ahashverosh gave Esther all of Haman's wealth. Esther, in turn, put Mordechai in charge of Haman's property.

But there was still one more thing to be done.

"My people will still be destroyed by the terrible decrees that Haman sent throughout the land," Queen Esther told the king. "Please make new decrees allowing the Jewish people to save themselves."

"You may write whatever you wish," the king told Esther, "and seal it with my royal ring."

A new decree was written. In it, Mordechai wrote:

On the 13th day
of the 12th month, called Adar,
the king hereby permits
the Jews of every city
to defend themselves.
They may attack anyone
who comes to harm them.

The Jews were happy. On the day Haman picked to destroy the Jews – the 13th of Adar – their enemies tried to attack them, but the Jews had gathered weapons and were ready for battle. On the 14th of Adar, the Jews rested from their battles.

In the city of Shushan, the Jews were given an extra day – the 14th of Adar – to continue the battle against their enemies. On the 15th of Adar, the Jews of Shushan rested from their battles.

Mordechai wrote down everything that happened. He sent letters to the Jews throughout the provinces of the king, telling them that those in villages and towns were to celebrate the 14th day of Adar as Purim. Those in towns and cities enclosed by walls, like Shushan, were to celebrate Purim on the 15th day of Adar.

Everyone was to celebrate Purim by having a great feast, enjoying themselves, sending wonderful foods to each other, and giving gifts to the poor. This was to be a tradition to be handed down for all generations.

Mordechai became a great man in Persia. He was greatly loved among the Jews because he always tried to do good for his people and worked hard to create peace among them.